WEATHER WATCH

Clouds

by Alice K. Flanagan

Look up at the clouds in the sky. What sizes and shapes do you see?

Many types of clouds can dot the sky.

There are several types of clouds. Each type has its own shape. Some types of clouds are higher in the sky than others.

During sunset, clouds can look colorful.

Some clouds look like big mountains in the sky. These clouds sometimes bring rain. They can also bring thunder and lightning.

The tallest and biggest clouds can bring thunder and lightning.

Some clouds look like feathers or horses' tails. These clouds are usually high up in the sky.

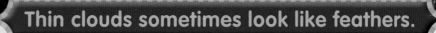
Thin clouds sometimes look like feathers.

Other clouds cover the sky like blankets or ocean waves. They have curly tops and make lots of neat shapes.

The tops of clouds can be seen from an airplane.

But what are clouds? Clouds are tiny drops of water in the air that have joined together.

These clouds are forming over the Atlantic Ocean.

Sometimes the drops become too heavy to stay in the air. Then they fall as rain. If the air is cold enough, the drops fall as snow.

Rain from these clouds is falling over the ocean.

Not all clouds bring wet weather. White, feathery clouds usually do not bring rain or snow. Dark clouds usually do bring rain or snow.

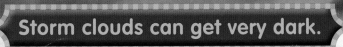

Storm clouds can get very dark.

Clouds bring more weather than just rain or snow. They can bring **tornadoes** and **hail**. Sometimes this weather causes **damage**.

A tornado comes down from a cloud.

Look up at the sky. Can you tell what type of weather the clouds will bring today?

Small, white clouds dot the sky.

Glossary

damage (DAM-ij): Damage happens if something is harmed. Hail can cause damage to a car.

hail (HAYL): Hail is tiny balls of ice that fall from the sky. When hail falls, you can see it on the ground.

tornadoes (tor-NAY-dohs): Tornadoes are swirling tubes of air that come down from the sky. Some clouds can bring tornadoes.

To Find Out More

Books

Bauer, Marion Dane. *Clouds*. New York: Simon & Schuster, 2004.

Day, John A. *The Book of Clouds*. New York: Sterling, 2005.

Rockwell, Anne. *Clouds*. New York: HarperCollins, 2008.

Web Sites

Visit our Web site for links about clouds: *childsworld.com/links*

Note to Parents, Teachers, and Librarians: We routinely verify our Web links to make sure they are safe and active sites. So encourage your readers to check them out!

Index

About the Author

Alice K. Flanagan taught elementary school for ten years. She has been writing for more than twenty years. She has written biographies and books about holidays, careers, animals, and weather.

On the cover: A large cloud covers the sky.

Published by The Child's World®
1980 Lookout Drive • Mankato, MN 56003-1705
800-599-READ • www.childsworld.com

ACKNOWLEDGMENTS
The Child's World®: Mary Berendes, Publishing Director
The Design Lab: Design and production
Red Line Editorial: Editorial direction

PHOTO CREDITS: iStockphoto, cover, 5, 7; Don Wilkie/iStockphoto, 3; Evgeny Kuklev/iStockphoto, 9; Irina Efremova/iStockphoto, 11; Damir Spanic/iStockphoto, 13; Oliver Hamalainen/iStockphoto, 15; Björn Kindler/iStockphoto, 17; Clint Spencer/iStockphoto, 19; Steeve Roche/iStockphoto, 21

Printed in the United States of America in Mankato, Minnesota.
November 2009
F11460

LIBRARY OF CONGRESS CATALOGING-IN-PUBLICATION DATA
Flanagan, Alice K.
  Clouds / Alice K. Flanagan.
    p. cm. — (Weather watch)
  Includes index.
  ISBN 978-1-60253-359-2 (library bound : alk. paper)
  1. Clouds—Juvenile literature. I. Title. II. Series.
  QC921.35.F55 2010
  551.57'6—dc22   2009030211